We're Going On!

The Collected Poems of Tom Wintringham

We're Going On !
The Collected Poems of Tom Wintringham

Edited by Hugh Purcell

smoke
STACK
BOOKS

In memory of O.J., Tom's eldest son who died in 2004, and with thanks to Lesley, Tom's daughter, without whom this collection would not have been possible.

Published 2006
by

STACK
BOOKS

Smokestack Books
PO Box 408, Middlesbrough TS5 6WA
Tel : 01642 813997
e-mail : info@smokestack-books.co.uk
www.smokestack-books.co.uk

Cover design and print by
James Cianciaruso
j.cianciaruso@ntlworld.com

Cover photograph of Tom Wintringham,
Madrigueras, Spain 1936

ISBN 0-9551061-0-9

Smokestack Books
gratefully acknowledges the support of
Middlesbrough Borough Council
and Arts Council North East.

Smokestack Books is a member of
Independent Northern Publishers
www.northernpublishers.co.uk

Contents

PART III : SPAIN (1936-7)

Introduction

Tom Wintringham was a soldier. During the First World War he was a motor-cycle dispatch rider ; in the Spanish Civil War he commanded the British Battalion of the International Brigade ; during the Second World War he was the driving force and inspiration behind the establishment of the Home Guard.

He was a revolutionary. A founder member of the Communist Party, he was one of the twelve Communist leaders gaoled for 'Sedition' in 1925. He edited the *Worker's Weekly*, helped launch the *Daily Worker* and was one of the first editors of *Left Review*. Expelled in 1938 from the Communist Party, Wintringham co-founded the Commonwealth Party and almost won a famous war-time by-election. His many books included *The Coming World War*, *Mutiny*, *English Captain*, *The Politics of Victory*, *People's War* and the best-selling *Your M.P.*

And he was a poet. When he was sixteen he called himself 'one of the genus veritabile vatum or the veritable race of poets'. Twenty years later in Spain, he referred to himself as 'the poet who had no time for poems because the miseries of the world shadowed by war "were miseries and would not let him rest"'. And yet it is clear that he did find time for poems. Uniquely, Wintringham wrote poetry on active service in two of the century's major wars. For him, the first was wholly unjustified, despite the heroism and camaraderie which it produced. The second was wholly justified, although it ended in painful defeat. Between these two wars lies a remarkable intellectual and poetic trajectory, and a unique body of poetry. This selection brings together, for the first time, the poems he wrote during a quarter of a century of high political drama and military adventure.

Tom Wintringham was born on 15 May 1898 into a prosperous Liberal family in Grimsby, Lincolnshire. His father was the town's senior solicitor, specialising in maritime law. His Uncle Tom had been a Liberal Member of Parliament, the only MP who has died literally on the floor of the House of Commons. His place in

Parliament was taken by his wife, Margaret, who became the first British woman MP (Nancy Astor was American).

Wintringham was educated at the first progressive school of the new century, Gresham's at Holt in Norfolk. Under the headmastership of G.W.S. Howson and then J.R. Eccles, the regime tutored an extraordinary number of boys who later became famous artists, scientists, musicians and poets. Gresham's must also number among its Old Boys more notorious Communists than any other school. First there was Tom Wintringham, then the KGB agent Cedric Belfrage followed by James Klugmann and Donald Maclean; Gresham's two outstanding poets were W H Auden and Stephen Spender, both Communist sympathisers in the 1930s.

Boys at Gresham's were taught to think for themselves and to take a holistic view of education that valued the sciences as much as the arts, the practical as much as the classical. Competitive sport, muscular Christianity, hierarchical discipline, were out. The influence on Wintringham lasted throughout his life. In later years he took as much pleasure writing poems as dismantling a motorbike, a versatility that women found very attractive. He was a linguist, lawyer, historian, scientist, writer, poet and soldier.

'When the Great War came', he wrote in 1937, 'I was torn between a half-understood idealist socialism and this fierce interest in fighting. But I was not quite so interested in war as I used to be because I had begun to write poetry. I was sixteen. The world was a muddle.' He enlisted in the Royal Flying Corps just after his eighteenth birthday but was prevented from flying by bad eyesight. Instead he joined the Second Kite Balloon Corps on the Western Front as a dispatch rider, his job being to collect dispatches thrown out of balloons tethered high over the rear trenches to provide information about the enemy. He wrote later that he was 'fooled into the incredibly blinkered patriotism of the spring of 1916, the Rupert Brooke, "Now God be thanked Who has matched us with this hour"'. It was not long, however, before he lost his idealism. This time it was the writer H.G. Wells who guided his feelings: 'He showed me that the misunderstanding, the injustice, the stupidity was world-wide. He also showed me that there existed revolt and rage against this stupidity, an eager seeking for a planned, clean, sensible society.'

Wintringham claimed later that he refused to apply for a commission: 'I couldn't be one of those responsible for the war; must be with the ordinary men, lousy and lumpy.' As a public school boy he cannot have had much contact with 'ordinary men', certainly not on equal terms, but now he was fighting with them with the fellow rank of private. He wrote to his mother : 'the men I meet here are openhearted, strong, capable of carrying the intolerable burden of industrial life in manhood without servility or blind obedience. But they have not the development of brain, of choice by reason, of rational vision'.

He would soon begin to study the 'rational vision' of Marx and Lenin. The Russian revolution of 1917 impressed him, particularly when it led to a peace treaty with Germany. He took part in a very minor 'mutiny', as he later called it with pride, over conditions in a hospital he was sent to with heavy flu. He discovered the iniquities of class, writing to his mother : 'Unless the nouveau riche and the business men are controlled then the upper class will fall to the guillotine'. In the trenches were planted the seeds of his communism.

In 1919 Wintringham went up to Balliol College Oxford, with a history scholarship. He joined the new Labour Club and edited its paper *New Oxford*. There he met Ralph Fox, later a novelist, Communist Party journalist and International Brigader (Fox was killed in Spain). Increasingly opposed to capitalism and convinced that the Great War had been 'an imperialist continuation of its fundamental properties' Wintringham began reading Marx.

Suddenly 'the world ceased to be a muddle; it could be understood by those who understand in order to change. That satisfied me'. Like many others, he believed that communism was the ideology whose time had come. With his keen sense of English history he also saw it as a culmination of what had passed - the Peasants Revolt of the fourteenth century, the Levellers and Diggers agitation during the Civil War and the Chartists of the nineteenth century were the revolutionary precursors of the imminent Communist overthrow of capitalism. Not that revolution would just happen. He quoted approvingly the saying of Freud: 'When we can see the anvil of fact, then we can use the hammer of will'.

Wintringham did not yet call himself a communist, though he may have attended the Unity Conference that launched the Party on 31 July 1920. A few weeks later he visited the new Soviet Union. Hearing Trotsky speak, meeting John Reed (author of *Ten Days that Shook the World*), checking English language scripts for Rusian radio and debating 'Futurism and seven other-isms, each less comprehensible than the first', he shared the euphoria of revolution. Moscow in 1920 was the practical affirmation of his faith in socialism, but he never returned.

Back in Britain he joined the Inner Temple and began studying for the Bar. He also joined the Communist Party (whose headquarters at 16, King Street, were close to the Inner Temple). Wintringham was one of a small group of university intellectuals in an overwhelmingly working-class organisation. Party friends included Rose Cohen, Eva Reckitt, Robin Page Arnot and Raji Palme Dutt. Brilliantly clever but famously manipulative, Palme Dutt (who was also at Balliol) was totally dedicated to the dictum that the end justifies the means. Palme Dutt and his future wife, a professional revolutionary from Estonia named Salme Murrik, were to exert a huge influence on Wintringham over the next fifteen years. They convinced him of the need for 'the ruthless sacrifice of self, of so-called moral scruples also'. If he was to join the vanguard of the revolution then he had to accept 'an iron discipline, a central body armed with extensive powers'. The end was communism; any means was justified.

For the next fifteen years Wintringham was a professional, dedicated - and optimistic - revolutionary. He was given the code name 'Lincoln' (he later used it as a pen-name) and became one of the 'young Turks' around Palme Dutt and Harry Pollitt. They were determined to turn the Party from a rag bag of street corner orators into a centralised, disciplined, Bolshevik Party. Its initial aim was to infiltrate the Labour movement and trade unions with the intention, in Lenin's words, 'of offering the Labour Party the right hand of friendship while leaving the left hand free for the knockout blow'. Or as an early Communist put it, 'first we put the Labour Party into office, and then, when they get into office, our first act is to kick them out'.

In February 1923 Wintringham became assistant editor of the Party's *Workers' Weekly*. The following year the editor, Johnny Campbell, was charged with Incitement to Mutiny for publishing an equivocal appeal to the armed forces not to support the state in industrial disputes: 'Form committees in every barracks, Smash capitalism, Refuse to shoot strikers in industrial disputes! Turn your weapons on your oppressors!' When the charges were dropped, the Conservatives accused the Labour Government of being soft on communism, and Ramsay Mac Donald resigned.

In the middle of the election campaign, police arrested Wintringham and Campbell at Wintringham's flat. Within a few days twelve of the Communist Party's leaders had been arrested on charges of 'Sedition' (Wintringham had written a pamphlet addressed to the armed forces : 'Use your arms on the side of your own class. Turn your weapons on your oppressors'). Two weeks later the *Daily Mail* published a letter supposedly from the general secretary of the Comintern, Zinoviev, apparently calling on the CPGB to set up cells in the armed forces. The Conservatives won the election, all the Communist leaders were imprisoned and Wintringham was sentenced to six months.

Three weeks after Wintringham was released, the General Strike began. What he did during the Strike is not clear, but he seems to have gone underground, possibly editing the *Worker's Bulletin* (the writing and distributing of which was a prison offence). The Strike was called off and the miners were eventually defeated, but to the CPGB it was an encouraging prelude to revolution. Wintringham asked rhetorically in *Workers' Weekly* on 6 June; 'Who is coming in to the Party that foresees as well as fights, whose policy and outlook was right and is right now ?' Party membership doubled that Summer to 10,000.

The Comintern, believing that the situation was ripe for Revolution, moved strategically to the Left, ordered an end to collaboration with Labour and the advance of the Party as the only true party of revolution. The Labour Party were class enemies, little better than social fascists. This 'Class Against Class' period of Communism was welcomed at first by the Party leadership but it isolated its members from the trade unions and the Labour Party. Wintringham was soon convinced that 'Class Against Class' was a mistake ; Leninist doctrine was for a united front. He wrote an article called 'Allies Are Needed for the Revolution' in the *Daily Worker* as early as 1932 and was criticised for his heresy. This was an unhappy period in Wintringham's life. He was not politically astute. He was undeniably a 'bourgeois intellectual' at a time when the Party was 'rigorously proletarian'. He needed to keep his head down.

Prematurely bald, the result he said of wearing a crash helmet throughout the Great War, his appearance was dominated by a large domed head over thin-wired spectacles. He dressed untidily, travelling around on a motorbike with rucksack and greatcoat, so that he looked like a professor down on his luck. His manner added to this impression; mild, bookish and unsociable. He belonged, he said, 'to a quiet writing desk or the clatter of a print shop, little rooms where committees met'. But appearances were deceptive. Like his acquaintance T.E. Lawrence he delighted in the technicalities of war. Come the revolution Wintringham would have been on the streets.

In 1923 Wintringham married Elizabeth Arkwright (probably the only foundation member of the Communist Party to have been educated at Roedean and Lady Margaret Hall, Oxford University). They had one surviving son Oliver. In 1929 Wintringham began a long affair with another Party member, Millie —, with whom he had a daughter Lesley. Although he returned to Elizabeth and Lesley was placed in a children's home, the affair continued and Millie changed her name to Wintringham.

In 1929 the Communist Party asked Wintringham to work-full time preparing Britain's first daily Communist newspaper, the *Daily Worker*. The paper, which was successfully launched on 1 January 1930, was soon selling 45,000 a day. By 1945 it was selling 100,000 copies a day.

In 1934 Wintringham became Secretary of the British Section of the Writer's International and founder editor of *Left Review*. Intellectuals were back in favour with the Communists after years of having to pretend they wore a cloth cap. Wintringham contributed poems, reviews and essays to *Left Review*, including 'Who is for Liberty ?'calling for a specifically English revolution :

'There is a tradition of freedom and the struggle for freedom that is fundamental in the development of this country, built into our lives and minds. This tradition has at times been neglected, avoided, rejected by revolutionaries. But it is our heritage. Roundhead, Whig, Radical – there have been versions of this idea. Freedom can only be made real to the extent that socialism is made real but there must be change and growth among revolutionaries. We must make our own those symbols and that heritage that are the British equivalents of 'Liberty, Equality, Fraternity', and the Marseillaise.'

In July 1935 the Seventh World Congress of the Communist International declared the end of Class Against Class and the beginning of the Popular Front. The international order was changing fast. The Soviet Union had joined the League of Nations and had cast off its isolation. An alliance of all social democratic parties was needed against the very real threat of German, Italian and Japanese Fascism and its appeasers in Britain. For Wintringham this policy change was more than another political manoeuvre; it was a reality he had been urging for three years.

By now Wintringham was establishing a reputation as the foremost, if not the only, Marxist writer on military strategy. He wrote *The Coming World War* (1935) and the next year *Mutiny : a Survey of Mutinies from Spartacus to Invergordon.* In early 1936 he became Military Correspondent of the *Daily Worker*, with almost immediate but far-reaching consequences.

In August 1936 Harry Pollitt, now General Secretary of the CPGB, asked Wintringham to go to Barcelona as the Party's representative or 'responsable'. The Civil War had just broken out and young foreigners, mostly socialists or communists, were gathering in this revolutionary centre. Wintringham also intended to cover the war for the *Daily Worker*. But he was most interested in putting together an 'international legion' (his phrase) of young communist fighters to defend the democratically elected, socialist, Republic against fascism. The historian Hugh Thomas wrote in *The Spanish Civil War* (1961) : ' it is possible that Wintringham deserves more credit than others for the International Brigades'. He travelled to Spain in August with the first ambulance unit paid for by the Spanish Medical Aid Committee. When he arrived in Barcelona he met young British communists who were there for the Worker's

Olympiad. They started recruiting for what they called the Tom Mann centuria and Wintringham wrote to Pollitt asking for volunteers. They were among the first of over 2,000 volunteer fighters who went to Spain from Britain over the next two years. More than five hundred of them were killed. For Wintringham they were an army of 'the free men of Europe' : 'It's the first battalion put together by English speaking people - the first since Cromwell's day - to be part of a people's army. It's as important as the New Model Army.'

The British Battalion of volunteer soldiers became part of the International Brigades that were formed in October. Wintringham was appointed Machine Gun Instructor at its base in Albacete. The following February he became Commander of the British Battalion and only a few days later, on 12 February, the Battalion went into battle for the first time near the Jarama river. Eventually the Republican Army, helped by the International Brigades, were victorious for the fascist troops were prevented from capturing the Madrid to Valencia road. But the first two days of the Battle of Jarama were a bloodbath with over 250 of the 400 British volunteers on 'Suicide Hill' killed, wounded or captured. Wintringham himself was wounded and withdrawn on the second day of fighting. In hospital he caught typhoid so that for nearly four months he was out of action. In June 1937, still not fully fit, he was posted as instructor to the Abraham Lincoln (American) Battalion. In August he rejoined the British Battalion, was wounded on the Aragon front and hospitalised for the second time.

By the time Wintringham was repatriated at the end of 1937, he was in serious trouble with the Comintern. When he was in Barcelona he had met a wealthy young American adventuress called Kitty Bowler. They soon became lovers and Wintringham encouraged her to write as a 'stringer' in Spain for the *Manchester Guardian*. In circumstances that were not unusual, for this was the height of Stalin's purges in the Soviet Union, she was arrested and interrogated as a 'Trotskyite spy' and later expelled from Spain. Although there was no truth in this charge Wintringham was ordered to end the relationship. He refused and was expelled from the Communist Party in July 1938. Wintringham eventually divorced Elizabeth and married Kitty in 1941. Their son Ben was born in 1947.

Spain was a watershed in Wintringham's life. In 1941 he summed up his experience and re-iterated the testament he had lived by since that war :

'Spain woke me up. Politically I rediscovered democracy, realising the enormous potentialities in a real alliance of workers and other classes, the power that can come from people working together for things felt and believed, when a popular front is not just a manoeuvre but also a reality. I was disgusted by sectarian intrigues and by the hampering suspicions of Marty and co....Two bullets and typhoid gave me time to think. I came out of Spain believing, as I still believe, in a more humane humanism, in a more radical democracy, and in a revolution of some sort as necessary to give ordinary people a chance to beat Fascism. Marxism makes sense to me, but the 'Party Line' doesn't.'

The moral that Wintringham took from Spain was that citizens would only fight a 'people's war', a guerrilla war to defend their country, if they thought it was a country worth dying for. This meant that the country had to belong to the people, had to be a socialist country. It also had to be a democratic one; patriotism was not enough. This became his credo, developed in his books *English Captain* (1939), *Deadlock War* (1940) and *How to Reform the Army* (1939), in which he called for 'an army of freemen available for service at a few hours notice'. 'This', he said, 'is part of a tradition going back over a thousand years to the 'fyrd' and 'wapentake' through the 'posse comitatus' and the assizes of arms, to the militia of Queen Elizabeth and the volunteers of the last century'.

In the summer of 1940, after the Low Countries and France had surrendered in the face of the Nazi blitzkrieg and the British Army had been evacuated from Dunkirk, Britons awaited their fate, sure that Hitler would order an invasion across the Channel. The Government appealed for Local Defense Volunteers. Over a quarter of a million men besieged police stations within twenty-four hours. This was Tom Wintringham's moment.

For the first time Wintringham's political convictions answered a public need. Like Orwell, Wintringham believed that war provided the best opportunity for a socialist revolution and that a revolution was necessary for fascism to be defeated. 'We are in a strange period of history', Orwell wrote,' in which a revolutionary has to be a patriot and a patriot has to be a revolutionary.' Wintringham's ability to tell people how to defend themselves, how to wage guerrilla war, was welcomed by a population expecting a Nazi invasion at any time. He was, in Orwell's words 'a notable voice in stemming the tide of defeatism'. He was a revolutionary patriot whose time had come. His political beliefs found a ready audience that summer when the national mood has been described as 'a collective aggression for change'. Wintringham was the prophet of the Home Guard. He was also a household name and the best-known proponent of guerilla war and do-it-yourself defense through a series of articles in *Picture Post* and the *Daily Mirror*, BBC talks and columns in *Tribune* and the *New Statesman*. In 1940 he published two books, *New Ways of War* and *Armies of Freemen* that together sold over one hundred thousand copies in a few months. While Churchill's deeply patriotic oratory called to mind an aged Henry V and Priestley was compared to that 'honester and true-hearted' man Falstaff, Wintringham's persona was his hero, the Leveller John Lilburne. His slogan in the *Daily Mirror* was: 'An Aroused People, An Angry People, An Armed People', and his pledge in *New Ways of War*: 'Knowing that science and the riches of the earth make possible an abundance of material things for all, and trusting our fellows and ourselves to achieve that abundance after we have won, we are willing to throw everything we now possess into the common lot, to win this fight. We will allow no personal considerations of rights, privileges, property, income, family or friendship to stand in our way. Whatever the future may hold we will continue our war for liberty'.

As the founder-director of the Guerilla Warfare Training School at Osterley Park he taught the rudiments of irregular war for civilians; rifle shooting and bomb making, street defense, camouflage and field craft. It may have looked a bit comic, it was certainly a bit desperate and luckily it was never put to the test. Wintringham's nickname was the 'red revolutionary' so it was not surprising that the War Office mistrusted him. They took over the Training School, moved it out of London and ignored him. He resigned in May 1941.

In fact Wintringham did have a political agenda though he scarcely taught it at Osterley. When he described the Home Guard in the preface of the Penguin edition of *English Captain* (1941) as 'a new sort of army', and he intended with this phrase a comparison with the New Model Army of the Civil War, he really meant a new kind of society - classless, meritocratic, and consensual in that it managed itself in a democratic way. And as his pledge at the end of *New Ways of War* clearly implied, this society was to be socialist.

When Germany invaded the Soviet Union and declared war on the United States a few months later, the threat of invasion was over and the role of the Home Guard more questionable. In any event Wintringham had moved on. 'Now what in hell can we do about this damned world ?' he asked. His answer was *The Politics of Victory* (1941). In it he called for a new popular front of discontented Marxists like himself and Labour voters who felt muzzled by their party's membership of the war-time coalition government. Encouraged by the activities of the 1941 Group, in the summer of 1942 he and the Liberal MP Richard Acland launched a new progressive political organisation, the Common Wealth party. Common Wealth won three by-elections before the end of the War. In February 1943 Wintringham himself very narrowly lost a by-election in the Edinburgh constituency of North Midlothian, polling 48% of the vote.

But when the Labour Party embraced Beveridge's plans for a welfare state it in effect stole Common Wealth's clothes and it refused any kind of alliance. For Common Wealth the result of the July 1945 general election was a foregone conclusion. Wintringham stood again, at Aldershot in Hampshire, and narrowly lost again (with a third of the vote), but only one Common Wealth candidate was elected to parliament. After the election, Common Wealth was disbanded as a political party. Wintringham joined the Labour Party but he said he did not want to stand again as a candidate. His revolutionary options, and energy, were expended.

A significant factor in the Labour Victory of 1945 was a little book called *Your M.P* (1944). A controversial and devastating indictment of the back-bench admirers of Hitler in the Tory Party, it was published by Victor Gollancz, and sold over 200,000 copies. The author ('Gracchus') was Tom Wintringham. It was vilified by the Tories. 'The book should be banned', said Beverley Baxter MP. 'It is muck spreading, a pack of lies and half-truths. And it is published by Gollancz - a Jew'. In terms of sales it was Wintringham's most successful book.

After the war Wintringham pronounced the world 'a lousy mess' and retired with Kitty to Edinburgh. He waited for a call back to public life but it never came. He died suddenly and unexpectedly while helping with the harvest on his sister's farm in Lincolnshire on 16 August 1949. It was a peaceful death for a very English revolutionary. Wintringham was convinced that few things in life could be achieved unless you were prepared to fight for them. He understood that socialism would not just happen. His activism changed from mutiny and strike in the 1920s, to the Popular Front in the 1930s, to the Home Guard and Common Wealth in the 1940s. In each decade he was in the vanguard of revolutionary socialism.

Wintringham belongs to a long line of English revolutionaries. Like John Lilburne he went to prison for his beliefs; like Oliver Cromwell's English captains he came from Lincolnshire stock and tried to bring about an English revolution; and like George Byron he was a poet who fought for a lost cause in a foreign country. He drew very consciously on the idea of an English radical tradition. The Popular Front gave him the opportunity to appeal to this specifically English heritage. The war cast him first in the role of revolutionary patriot, an inspirer of another army of free men; and then as a new kind of revolutionary socialist, as the co-founder of Common Wealth. Wintringham believed, as the Digger Gerrard Winstanley wrote 300 years before, 'What other lands do, England is not to take pattern of'.

A Note on the Poems

Tom Wintringham was an occasional poet. He wrote occasionally, in the quiet interstices between one series of dramatic events and the next - in prison, on leave, in hospital, in bed. And he wrote for occasions - the Armistice, Empire Day, the conception of his daughter, the release of Dimitrov. His poems were written in the margins of a busy public life of action and external conflict. He was the poet 'who had no time for poems'. He made little attempt to promote his work and he never collected it for publication (only a dozen of these poems were published in his lifetime).

During the First World War he carried in his jacket a little 'commonplace book', in which he noted down in pencil a hundred pages of poetry, including Yeats, Arnold, Brooke and Flecker as well as notes for poems of his own. Much of his poetry has this unfinished, hurried character; they sometimes feel like notes for poems, extracts from an unfinished conversation with part of himself and with other writers. One reason why his poems from Spain are better known than the others is that they were collated by the faithful Millie, passed round a group of fellow Communist poets like Sylvia Townsend Warner and offered for publication.

Typically, Wintringham's poetry proceeds by way of dialectical argument between a series of opposite abstractions (Nature and War, History and Agency, Prison and Freedom, Then and Now, Sex and Death, Democracy and Fascism). Even the love poems are constructed in this way ('water and fire', 'air and loam', 'beauty' and 'need', desire and duty). Love, he wrote, should be 'dialectical with anger'.

He wrote with the material to hand, about immediate experience. But he was less interested in describing the way the world looked than in exploring what it meant. He was concerned to explore the relationship between ideas and facts, between the Ideal and the Real, the blueprint and the workbench, the manifesto and the political practice.

The poems which Wintringham wrote between 1914 and 1919 tell the story of one young man's transformation, from the militaristic raptures of 'The Funeral of Lord Roberts' and the public school-boy bellicosity of 'Mine Sweepers', Lofoden Light' and '1915' to a growing sense of dread ('Utterby Pines') and the anti-war sentiments of 'A Fat Man...', 'To Some Englishmen' and 'Awakening'. The changes are recorded in the loosening of the rhymes and the increasingly varied line-lengths. Where the juvenilia is heavy with second-hand gestures - archaic diction, capitalised abstractions and classical references - the poems written in France are awake to the sounds of modern war ('Mutter and thud and shudder, pulse and pause / The guns are waking and warring over the hill' ; 'ever incessant, crescent and clamorous runs... the curse of the crowded guns').

The frequent invocation of the English countryside was partly, no doubt, the pastoral escape of a homesick young soldier. Anticipating his own death in 'Armour' he tries to remember the beauty of Lincolnshire in spring, to escape the 'sulphur stink', 'poisonous weeds, and the dust, and dung' of the trenches. It is partly - as in the poetry of Edmund Blunden - a way of representing the War as 'unnatural' and therefore inhuman. But the repeated and violent contrasts between the natural world and modern warfare ('The ridge that was pulp in April, bare in May / Is caught in a net of delicate green and gold, / Over our dead the children's flowers sway') also feels like a growing repudiation of the values of a public-school education and the political system that legitimised the war.

Unlike Wilfred Owen, Wintringham did not record the physical extremes of conditions on the Western Front. His poems are not satirical or protesting like Sassoon's. Rather, like Edward Thomas and Ivor Gurney, he addresses a growing understanding that England was being changed forever by events in France. On the one hand, 'Youth' and the 'great dead'; on the other, 'a fat man with false teeth, who tells lies for his living'; 'the blood-blackened past' against 'Black tyranny, and gold'.

By the end of the war Wintringham was looking for a more contemporary vocabulary, one extensive enough to include the forces of Death and the armies of Life. He found it in the world of science and industry, specifically in the working of metal. After 1919, the 'gallant buttercups' and 'cloud-shadows on the corn' are replaced by the hard, industrial vocabulary of 'dynamos', 'lathe', 'gasometer', 'concrete', 'pistons, crankshaft-web and crankshaft-throw'. One poem, 'The Test' (with its epigraph from *Principles of Aero-Engine Design*) uses the word 'crankshaft' three times.

Several years before Auden's *Poems* and *The Orators*, Wintringham was seeking to import the language of science and modern industry into English poetry. (At the same time, Wintringham continued to use archaisms long after they had ceased to be accepted practice among his contemporaries). The result may seem dated today, although in fact it long pre-dated the 'Pylon Poets' of the 1930s. Wintringham's brother Charles was an exact contemporary of Auden at Gresham's School and Wintringham's papers include an exercise book of Auden's schoolboy poetry, in his own hand, suggesting that the young Auden may have met Wintringham in the 1920's.

The most extreme example is 'The Immortal Tractor'. It was written at the height of the Class Against Class period, when communist literature was at its most combative and polemical, not to say hysterical (compare McDiarmid's 'Second Hymn to Lenin'). Even the Palme Dutts were not impressed. Wintringham asked them for their opinion, saying that he had only received 'an embarrassed answer, a "we're thinking about it"' from the *Daily Worker*. Dutt told him to change the first line (originally 'I have heard Lenin speak'), adding that Salme, his formidable wife, thought Wintringham wrote his poems on too large a canvas.

But the rhetoric is not necessarily of Soviet provenance. The Proletkult movement had made almost no impact on the British left and Soviet poetry was largely unpublished in Britain at that time (even Mayakovsky's work was not available in English until the 1940s). Anyway, Wintringham's fascination with fast machines - motorbikes, cars and planes - was second only to his infatuation with women. He wrote a number of analytical articles for *Labour Monthly* about modern weapons and warfare. Machines were a characteristic product of the modern world and an emblem of the future. They represented collective human achievement, hard historical determinacy and individual human will (Lenin, Dimitrov and Rakosi). In 'Speaking Concretely', the individual elements are moulded into a mass, reinforced by steel and solidified to make concrete, no doubt unlovely but certainly useful.

'Against the Determinate World' is the most ambitious of Wintringham's pre-Spanish poems, dialectically opposing the languages of science and traditional poetry. It explores the tension between History and the individual, reason and feeling, science and politics. The laws of nature pull one way, the lure of nature pulls another. Beauty and love and freedom may be human constructs, subjective and illusory, but they are the 'means' by which History achieves its ends.

Unlike most of the combatants in the Spanish Civil War who wrote poetry, Wintringham was already a published poet and an experienced soldier ('twenty years ago I knew war's face'). Unlike those non-combatants who wrote rhapsodic, romanticising verse about the heroic struggle of the Spanish Republic and of the International Brigades, Wintringham had no illusions about war. He wrote the first poem, 'We're Going On !' within three weeks of arriving in Spain, in September 1936. It is framed by a clear-eyed purpose ('We're going on', 'What it's all for', 'our choice'). But it also acknowledges the brutal realities of modern warfare ('poison-gas, shell-shock, the mud death', 'Death means the corpses warm alive when buried').

Wintringham was unsentimental about the human costs of war ('Love is not / Timeless. Love is over / for thousands who went out this summer weather / and found the feast set, and the feast was death'), as he was about his own mortality ('after victory, we shall be forgotten / as men forget seed-grain, harrowing, dung'). Even in 'International Brigades', where he may have been forgiven a bit of political rhetoric, he resisted the temptation to sloganise ('Liberty / is a silly word, in this flat life, and used / Usually by a Lord Chief Justice. It smells of the last century.')

The poems he wrote in 1937 are increasingly personal, desperate. Wintringham sent 'Poem in The Summer of 1937' to Kitty before he went into action, pinning a copy into his passport so she would receive it in the event of his death. By the time he wrote 'Monument', he had been wounded twice and almost died of typhoid. The victory of the Republic was no longer assured. And Wintringham was beginning to question aspects of the Comintern's operation in Spain. The poem tries to imagines post-war Spain, when the victorious Republic would honour the International Brigades. The monument would be a beacon for the future, a statement of 'Spain's Unity, happiness, strength', but it would be built - like the poem - on 'memories of death' and all the war's many cruelties and atrocities.

Tom Wintringham was at the centre of so many of the key events of his day. His poems read like a series of expanded footnotes to the history of his time - public-school boy patriotism, the First World War, the road to Moscow, the roads to Spain. The poems which he wrote in Spain are clearly his most important, distinguished by a political maturity and a quite distinctive and assured poetic voice. They deserve to be remembered as among the most significant and memorable of that conflict, the poems of a soldier for whom 'there is war in the world and little music'.

A Sparrow; at 6 am

O songster most impertinent
Why wakest thou the world
Before the sun-God's bow is bent
His flaming dawn-darts hurled?

O smallest singer, e'en the dawn,
Why troublest thou my dreams?
You've seen before the flaming morn'
Apollo's brilliant beams,

You know the moon will softly sink
Behind the tree tops tall,
You know the sun is on the brink,
Of rising, filling all,

With carmine-tinted glory
And zenith's deepening blue
Re-tell it not in story-
A sunrise is not new.

March 1914

The Funeral of Lord Roberts

Stillness and shaded lights
And the low muffled murmur of the drums
So the most perfect of an Empire's knights
To his last vigil comes.

All war shall cease, but may there never cease
Warriors, as he was warrior, for the right.
Peerless in war, he gave an Empire peace
A captain, too, of courtesy, a very gentle knight.

December 1914

Mine Sweepers

Out beyond the shallows where are white waves racing,
Leaping up and laughing, swinging in to shore,
Far upon the deeper seas a darker storm is pacing
Darker than all tempests that have burst on us before ..

Little recking tempest, toil and life are one to us
Flame and flood and steel and storm, deep-sea dark and grey
These we knew aforetime - now Death's self has come to us
Lurking in the shadows of the slow sea-sway.

These we knew aforetime, met their might and mastered it,
Hunting the sea-meadows from the Foreland to the floe
Blindfold through their blackness we made our way
                                        - and afterwards
To chance upon our death-stroke where sunlit ripples go!

Far beyond the sunrise there are strange seas flowing,
Distant are the waters where we lead the Last Crusade,
Troy, Lemnos, Mytilene – these shall tell you of our going
As bastions to your battlements and scabbard to your blade.

Swiftly come the ships through the great seas plunging,
Swinging through the sea-scud in majesty and pride,
Swiftest the destroyers, and like a rapier's lunging
Their on-rush comes in anger down the tumult of the tide.

Proudly come the ships through the whipped seas swinging,
Cleaving through the combers that rasp along the side,
Silent in their strength until the battle-bolts are singing,
And they go in flame and fury down the reddened reeking tide.

Proudly come the ships yet they must follow after us :
We sweep their paths to battle – hold they well the paths we've made
For the seeds of death and terror are in flower, and we, the harvesters
Must reap and pay for reaping, as the English ever payed.

February 1915

Lofoden Light

Here, where the white waves lash their sudden spray
    Flame-like in fury, 'gainst the sombre rocks,
    Where the hill-shaking heaving great surge-shocks
Beat out their thunder-chorus, here the way
Leads on my beacon. And here, when the new day
    Fringes the East, the moan of seas that roam
    Rises, and roars: the chant of the Maelstrom,
Then my light marks the whirlpool, gleaming grey.

Whether nearby the dreaming sunlit sea
Goes ripple, ripple, ripple, silently,
Or the lightning leaps, like an angel's sword
    Striking at earth, ever my light burns clear –
    Behind, the black cliffs gloom, like great sin is fear
    While life and death dance thro' the open fiord.

29 May 1915

Utterby Pines

I think the pagan gods, out-cast and old,
Haunt these old woods. Strange shadows have I found,
Have seen young saplings swaying without sound,
And briars bending wind-less to the mould;
    As if their great robes, sweeping fold on fold,
Whispering not, their colours shadow-drowned,
Had bent the sighing branches to the ground
Or broken them for touching, overbold.

Tower set with shimmer of marble, girdled round
With singing streams, and walled with sunlit stone;
--- Such their white temples once, when worship-crowned;
Now the black pines sway with a shuddering moan
Over their ghosts. Such bitterness around
I dare not enter these dark woods alone.

June 1915

1915

There can be never silence. I have heard,
When, after a long ecstasy of rain
Great trees dream whisperless, and dancing flowers
Are held in thrall to the rainbow's poised spell
That binds the breeze to silence --- I have heard
The sea's wave-mantled voices moaning
Far off, beyond the sunset

        Even so
When wrong walks naked and with brazen face,
When Death grips Life with hands of blasphemy,
And Murder marches 'neath a banner of God ---
The voice of a world's sorrow, not despairing,
That makes our dead the promise, "Ne'er again"!

July 1915

'Thoughts come like shadow unseen ...'

Thoughts come like shadow unseen, quietly from behind;
Or as the rustle of streams, that ever do dreamily
Drift through the heat, may come most stealthily
To one half-sleeping; as the hot slow wind
Creeps quite unnoticed up, without a sign
Save for the ripple of trees and sway of corn,
Or as the first faint glimmer of new morn
Tinges unmarked the whole horizon's line,

So come my thoughts to me, but ere I feel
The whisper of a thought's wings on my cheek
Beauty to beauty in my dreaming steal :
All loveliness of thought, how ere it speak
Plainly in joy or hidden sorrow through
- All beauty in the thought, and thoughts of you.

June 1915

'Within my heart ...'

Within my heart the hails of memory
Seem a long temple where the grey ghosts wheel,
Pillared by dreams that Time has deigned fulfil
And hung with rustle of thoughts for tapestry ---
Thoughts flooding like echoes over a murmuring sea
From black cliffs slowly flowing to and fro.
Amid this shadowy unrest you go,
And where you go dreams the still soul of me.

Friend of the flowers, and comrade of the sunlight,
I would have given you fairer throne than this.
With songs of banners of flame to burn till night
Came, and our songs were ended. But behold
you are far off ... and the grey hours are cold ...
What should my songs be, but old memories?

April 1916

'When Death's Swift Fingers ...'

For F.J.T.

When Death's swift fingers close about my throat,
And I forget cloud-shadows on the corn
Wind in the elm trees, silver of the dawn,
And scent of the dream flowers that round me float:-
When through the robing purple of the night,
or through the great white gateways of the morn,
I pass and wait, without you and forlorn,
At some far glimmering limit of the light -

I think that if just then you thought of me,
If even in your dreams a memory came
Of the strong bonds that held us, of the flame
Your eyes knew, and the quiver of your hand
Gainst mine - I think that God would understand
And for your sake allow me to go free.

1916/1917

Grainsby Hills

Oh fair child-face that I followed and found
Only in sleep, and the dreams that lie
Where the hills with a ripple of woods are crowned,
And the winds and the rabbits go scuttering by ---
Child-face I have watched for and loved so long
Will you not turn to me, hear my song?

Out alone in the little valley
Secret and silent, beyond the trees,
Where the slow winds flower-scented daily,
You came on the wings of a wandering breeze
When I wanted someone to walk with me,
Or lie in the sunlight and talk with me,
And laugh at the tumbling bumble-bees.

I half remember the touch of fingers
That brushed on mine as we tramped the hills,
There comes a glimpse of your face, that lingers
Beyond dream-barriers, laughter fills
All my memory, laughter flowing
A silken rivulet silver-blowing
From all my memory of you spills.

Why do you hide in the shadows so long,
Will you not turn to me, hear my song?

Savy sous Aubigny, August 1916

Armour

Harlots, it may be, go to Hell,
Princes to Paradise,
Or their souls may pass to the delicate grass,
Squirrels or snakes or lice;
Wherever you go, o soul alone,
Beyond my pulses' strain,
You shall not strive to keep alive
Memory, which is : Pain.

Magdalen walks in heaven forgiven
Borgia writhes in the sulphur stink,
While Luther and Leo squabble in limbo,
(And they're getting tired of you there, I think)
But you, o Soul who gave your whole
Life to love's treachery
You shall not turn, afraid, too late,
Shudder the curtains, beat the gate,
Plead or promise or cringe or wait
In grey despair Death's mastery.

Lo, I may die 'neath some grey sky
Among the northern hills,
Or where the swinging sea-gulls go
Above the grey Thames' listless flow,
Or where the Severn spills
Gay waves adown the Devon shore,
Or on some scented Norfolk moor
That gorse with colour fills.

So, when the stricken last sense fails,
Cut free from hope of sun,
Nor strive to pass Pain's swaying veils;
Away! Your dreams are done.

Swift, ere Their hands can snatch a hold
And you are chained to Death,
Free from Man and the Might above
Swing out to the little hills you love
Where friendship wandereth.

You must go down to a Lincoln lane,
- Pray God I die in Spring!
You must list to a bird's song once again
As of old; you must learn to sing.
If you can praise as the field-lark praises
If you go soaring, lissom of wing,
God will not turn from that chain of daisies
To see the paths you have searched among,
The poisonous weeds, and the dust, and dung.

Le Hamel, January 1917

Dawn Near Vimy

Mutter and thud and shudder, pulse and pause
The guns are waking and warring over the hill.
Swings a falcon, some small beast in his claws,
The air is still.
The ridge that was pulp in April, bare in May
Is caught in a net of delicate green and gold,
Over our dead the children's flowers sway.
Daisies and gallant buttercups carpet the way
And the broken trenches hold.
While ever incessant, crescent and clamorous
      runs,
On the breath of the summer morning, the
  curse of the crowded guns.

Vimy, 1917

Below Vimy

Shadow's sharp-edged. The stamping of great flashes
Is cracking and snapping the tracery of night;
While the moon walks silvery
Aloof and quiet and caring naught,
And the stars die slowly, in the slow march of the light.

Mutter, thud and shudder, pulse and aching pause again,
The guns awake to anger; paling Heaven shakes;
Crescent as a rising storm
Incessant as the raving seas
The crowded guns are cursing, while faint dawn breaks.

Neuville St Vaast, July 1918

'A Fat Man...'

A fat man with false teeth, who tells lies for his living
Told youth that war was making a man
of him;
Youth smiled, well remembering.

Courchelette, October 1918

Awakening

Victory, giving me
Colour and sound and scent,
What can you give to these
Who hear not song or breeze?
Only the grey weeds grow
Above them, and the slow
Long months march wearily;
Are they content?

The clamoured curses die,
True hearts have rest at last,
But still a few men hold Black tyranny, and gold,
Over man's work and will;
Our law and prophets still
With trick and treachery
Cling the blood-blackened past.

They will not rest, who lie
In broken lands and bare,
Till we destroy that goad,
Till we fling down that load
Of fatness for the few
Building our world anew
In living loyalty
To the great dead lying there.

Cambrai and Tortequenne, 1918

To Some Englishmen

With the force of twisted phrases you urged to curse and kill
"For right and faith and freedom" –
your call is echoing still.
Paid is the price, and made the peace,
But still your hands are hot
To choke the mother and the babe, till starving
bodies rot.

Above our dead in Picardy the children's
flowers play,
Golden the gallant buttercups, blood-red
the poppies sway,
But your hearts hold red lust and gold,
and the unborn shall grow
To curse us for your cowardice, who
starved a stricken foe.

Newton Abbott VAD, January 1919

To Margaret, in Her Fifth Summer

Our wise and friendly trees will stand
To watch you on your English way,
I do not know the path you've planned,
Nor what the promise of the day;
Only I know that my thoughts go
About you where you walk or play.

I know not if far seas will sing,
Or bending branches whisper you,
Or if the rebel breeze will bring
From overseas a kiss for you
Only I know not long ago
I kissed a small French miss for you.

Chateau de Bouvigny, June 1918

Margaret

Oh, laughter is a little word, and laughter is a little thing,
But when the fretting viols sing, or silver-throated hidden bird,
That only in the night is heard, for stylus low-murmuring,
I never feel that song has half the magic swiftness, and the swing
That lifts my heart on sun-lit wing, when very little children laugh.

Newton Abbott, December 1918

To My Mother

There are flowers in your garden that I cannot call to memory,
Many of the names of them I never knew at all
But I wish I was among them now, in rain and sunlight / shimmering,
In the silver evening, before the shadows fall.

There are flowers in my heart that I could not cut and press / for you,
Faded and forgotten now, lost beyond recall,
Idle thoughts and simple that I sought to drape and / dress for you
In easy songs and happy as a bird's clear call.

But you will know these flowers of mine, for in the / secret heart of
me
You dwelt to keep my soul alive, behind the dusk / dream wall,
You will have seen them swing and shine, whose haunting / ghosts are
part of me,
And --- Spring is breaking Winter that made them fade / and fall.

Newton Abbey, December 1918

'Aspens in the Autumn …'

Aspens in the autumn, quiet, wan, whisperless
Edged with sliding moon light, without glow, without gleam,
These hold the dream, the memories of mystery,
That fill your eyes with shadows, o friend of long ago.

Leaf to the leaf below tells very wistfully
Old songs and secrets, that we shall never know:
The branches crouch and quiver so … …
As if the moonlight were a river
That ripples ever-round and through
Silver of branch, and steel, and blue ----
Do you not know? These things are you.

Humberstone, August 1919

Balliol College, Oxford

I have seen a dynamo working

And I have smelt a gasometer
That is why I cannot accept your
            comparison
            of city lamps
   To stars-
Possibly also I have heard too many
      Of the gasometers of God,
      Felt too few of his dynamoes.

   1919

Against the Determinate World

The shadows lift, and the silver tree
That stands by Trinity Gate
In the breath of the dawn is dancing free,
Dancing smoothly and beckoning me:
An old book's weight
(Solemn, dusty) slips from my knee.

Folly man, folly! Let it go and get away!
Shout to the sunrise that the whipping winds are loose;
Run through the shadows, long and cool and clover-crisp,
Out to the great hills, clean with the day.

Urgency – and impotence –
Of atoms wheeling on their way
Mock you, with their thought-pretence;
While hooded forces bind and bend
Brain and body to an end
That is empty and ultimate – and yet lure you to believe!

This you know, this you feel, this you dream – they all are one;
Tenseness of the stopping hawk and sleekness of the lissom earth,
Pain and striving of man's sense to give the clamant Beauty birth,
And yon white cloud's wide immanence –

Watch the intricate atom-pattern!
Stated, fixed by Law of Chance,
Changeless in its shifting dance,
Changing throughout Permanence ….
Folly man, folly! Let it go and get away
          Out to the plough-land,
     chalk and heather,
          turf and clay;
               You shall leave

Consciousness of self and sex and thought and hope and all desire,
Nor know the gallant sun a star, nor name his laughing passion "fire",
But free from chains of space and date, and stripped of clamouring
                                                    want or will,

    Sleep
      in the sunlight,
    Sleep there,
      quiet,
        on the hill.

And sleep shall wash your memory clean of all things felt and all
                                                    things seen,
And all that ere your soul has heard shall be the singing
                                                    woodland bird
    That greets your waking, from the green
    Of branches sunlight slips between,
Singing old dreams that now you cannot follow,
Nor touch with questing fingers of the mind,
Yet cannot quite forget, in the hill's wide hollow,
Like an old song's tune, with forgotten words to find.

.. ..

To seek, to find, to prove ….
Oh – conquest, passion and high-hearted comradeship,
And the splendour of Man's strength, unwearying,
That accepts its blindness to the hands that move
Behind the frosts that shatter, winds that tear –
    Though now you cannot share
    In these, and play your part
    With a believing, with a burning heart,
    Yet Earth is still most fair

In this her seeming. Let's accept her lure:
We will pretend Life matters, 'Love' exists;
This fresh stream, 'crystal-pure'
Shall be the first of singers once again!
Not two bare elements, mixed with insect-life,
Each thrilling with the eternal ion-strife
That knows not victory, nor end nor pain.

(Very blue, very deep, very sweet
Is the pool of the sunlit air;
Under our feet the eyeless earth-worms creep;
They are blind, blind, blind,
Yet the magic sun is kind to them,
Without its gifts they die.
We are blind – but why should we care?)

For is not the sun then a God? Lo, he has marched
Swifter than dreams run on the skein of sleep,
He has torn the veil from the face of the passionate sky,
He has lit the clouds, he has coloured with fantasy
The gates of the morning, and broken the shadows apart,
Scattered and torn and destroyed them. Now swinging high,
He has set his peace upon earth, and his peace in your heart

Beyond question or pain.
You can turn now, go down,
You can meet men again,
You can take up your part
In the web of the doom that was woven before the earth cooled,
Before life was born
That enfolds though it cannot withhold you, that cannot be torn,
Whereof whim may alter the means, but will cannot alter the end,
Nor knowledge forfend.

It is written. Go down!

Moscow, 10 December 1920

Acceptance

I would turn traitor if I could,
And beauty-monger to the bourgeoisie ;
But the eyes of men who died in the dark
Do not forget me.

I would go back to a fair land,
And believe in the things I see;
But these were my friends. They believed, and died;
They will not let me.

Moscow, January 1921

The Cage

Heavy the burden we bear, whose minds are groping
Through mist of knowledge and darkened paths of thought,
Heavy the burden of fear, and the burden of hoping
Lest fear should hold us alive, and our souls be caught.

And words are stronger than we, strong and enchaining;
They straighten the tendrils of thought, they change desires
Into ink on paper page, with spaces remaining
To remind of unsayable things. Our words are wires

Of the cage where our minds walk ever, for ever pursuing
Freedoms the future promises, could we but find
Flame of the perfect words for our dream and our doing,
So that all men might see; but men are blind,

And we are still seeking for speech. Yet this we know;
Because we are dumb we are blind, and all men are so.

1923

Revolution

Can you not feel it? The long tide stirring,
The people passing, pausing, returning,
Swaying and surging in the cold wet streets?
And the fear in the faces of the fat? And the burning
Hope in the eyes where, terrible in hopelessness,
Lonely and cold a ghost of hunger sat?

Men will remember the past and its defeats;
Men will remember their dreams trodden underfoot
When they went in to the mills, to the docks, to the deep sea,
To the mines where the black dust gleams,
Or scarred the coloured hills with a grey plough –
Man's work
And boy's hopes, boy's dreams.

Men will remember!

The steel of their wills pointed by bitterness
And all their longing to master earth, to make,
(Now caught and constrained in a network of weariness,
Stifled by monotony, sameness, littleness)
These shall be strong in them, these shall awake
To a light, to a fire, to a bright fire's restlessness,
To a crackling anger.
        A promise will not slake
The passion of their courage, nor a "great man" break
The pressure of their urgency. Neither lies nor laws
Will hold them or hinder them or give them pause.

There will be a stirring, like a trembling of the earth,
And men will remember, singing in the streets
Where machine-guns rattle or a cracked drum beats,
That beyond the battle, the mourning, the slain,

The numb crouched agony of wounded in the rain,
There is power for them, freedom, security, friendliness,
Loveliness and laughter made sane and sweet and clean again
And beginning of a new world's birth.

1925

In the Garden

In the garden there came a snake
Whispering through the coloured grass :
The straight spears of the grass would make
A shivering bow as it went past .

When there was morning in the skies,
And the cold trees stood grey and tall,
I saw its raised head, and its eyes,
And strange sway of its body's coil.

Then I remembered : in my sleep
I had felt its head touching my knee;
I had felt the weight of its coils creep
Across my body's secrecy.

Why do my thoughts go twisting back,
However I guard them, to that snake ?
Night is a jungle-pool, creepy and black –
Adam ! I am afraid ! Afraid !

H M Prison Wandsworth, 1926

When Beauty Walks

When Beauty walks among men
She wears a wedding dress
And hides her eyes from the passers-by,
And her limbs' loveliness.

I have seen her – eyes that are bright with life,
Wing of a wheeling bird –
She sent me back to my trench again
Without a word.

When Beauty and Man lie down together
- They have been in love so long! -
Some other singer than I must make
Their wedding song.

H M Prison Wandsworth, February 1926.

In Haunted Cell

I never sought you in my thoughts,
Looking them through for lavender,
But often, past an opening door,
I seemed to see your shadow stir,
And hear the rustle of your dress.

I followed you along the paths
That memory tends within my mind,
There was no track of dancing feet,
Though sometimes on the wind I'd find
An echo of your tenderness.

But when I turned to face the tasks
That must be ours, before the tide
Of battle-years has done with us ---
I found you standing by my side
In loyal strength and loveliness.

H M Prison Wandsworth

Before Prison

I have known pride and power,
Seen under leaning wings
Village and city flower –
Queer, tiny, petalled things! –
I know the lilt of the tune
That a great car sings.

And I have lain with my love.

I have known fear, defeat,
Found dead my first-born son,
Found changeling love a cheat,
Lost youth, lost health, let run
Lust's snake across my brain;
And I've known pain.

These you can shut from me
By the prison gate;
But my love's loyalty
And comrades' fellowship
And my hate
Of your wars and your lies and your laws –
These I keep!

1925 and 1932

Remembering Prison

What is my liberty? It is the memory
Of chalk hills and meadow spaces,
Of the coloured and stirring sea,
Of a trout-stream that races
Broken silver in shallows
Soft shadows,
Of the rhythm of steel and of wings,
Of riding at speed that stings
Nerves, eyes, to arrogant mastery,
Of a babe's finger that clings
To mine
For the first time,
And of love, and friends' faces.

1933

The Immortal Tractor

Lenin was speaking. Careful, searching, keen,
His comrades heard him. Words became flame -
Not the white furnace-hunger, nor the light
Of guns that curse at night -
Flame at the heart of a vast machine,
Sparks small as steel can measure, strong alone
By striking thought, the mist of thought, to action :
Petrol to power. Words had grown
Electric, surely placed at the millionth fraction
Of time, to leap, explode, become
The pulse's drum,
The living, lifting, and life-giving factor
In the steel strength of the Immortal Tractor.

- Petrograd, 1917 -

The hates and fears have taken spears
To kill the dawn;
Panic and pride are on their side,
The Khirghiz and the Cossacks ride
Against the dawn –
    Hark to the hoofs of Yenghiz Khan !
    Ask, ask of Samarkand,
    Hindu, Kurd, or Turcoman,
    Was there ever a finer fighting-man ?
    The Khirghiz and the Cossacks come . . . .
In Petrograd a cracking drum
Summons the Red Guard to the street.
Lenin's words beat
With the rhythm of the factory, the red heat of the forge,
Explosive as the dynamite that cuts a mountain gorge.
Lenin is speaking, and the workers go
Through blood, mud, snow,
Through fear, lies, hate;

And the Cossacks hesitate;
They don't quite know . . . .
And Kerensky hesitates
At the stamping city's gates
-            Petty little posturing coward of an actor !
Shall he hide ?   Shall he fight ?   Shall he run? –
He decides. He deserts. But before his flight's begun
The armies hear the rumour of a rattling Tractor,
Pulling the guns up, cleaving, heaving,
Hurrying a city out, calling, hauling
All the life of Petrograd, breast and limb and brain,
To shake the world, and break the world – and make the world again!
- Leningrad, 1927 -

Here is the Plan,
Here is the greatest task ever faced by man.
Lenin is dead. But his words are living;
Lenin is living - every word a spark
Driving the great Tractor through the desert and the dark,
The million-powered Tractor, plunging on to victory -
By sacrifice and suffering, and all the unforgiving
Struggle to keep straight the track, thundering to victory -
Ploughing a furrow that is five years' deep ;
Ploughing the past under. The future will reap.
- London, 1933 -

Lenin is speaking. All who hear him know
Here, too, a Tractor's building, and will grow;
Here, in the cities where the cold fog kills,
In the ploughless valleys, on the blank, bare hills,
'Mid the famine of the mines and the phthisis of the mills,
We are moulding, forging, shaping the steel of our wills
Into pinions, into pistons, crankshaft-web and crankshaft-throw,
We are building Lenin's Tractor. It will grow.

1931 and 1933

Earth, Air, Fire and Water

--- Beauty was born when these came true,
But never before, dear Beauty's daughter,
Was a woman fire all through.

Yet passion with peace in your heart is married
To beget life and renew;
In our love that leapt, and our love that tarried
I have won life in you.

1930

We Quarrel So About Politics

When she changes, from your lover,
To harvest-headed lioness,
The days of lazy love are over.
Is that loss?

Sure, there was kettle-comfort then,
And beauty in soft heelless shoes.
Now beauty battles lash-tail … When
-- Win, lose --

There's ever-human need to feel,
Grow, see, do, sleeplessly enduring
New tempering and new edge to steel,
The true ring

Of the metal's lacking if we lack
Love dialectical with anger:
Love hammer-matrix, parry-attack,
As strangers stronger.

1934

Be to Your Lover

Because there is war in the world and little music,
Because there is hunger where the harvest spills,
Because of the children with old, thin, dull faces,
And the netted thoughts, and the thought-netted wills,
In the storm-clouded hours we seize for loving
Before the shells begin
Be to your lover as the bow moving
Is to the violin.

This is your strength to act, not need's fulfilment
This is your armoury, not just your home;
This makes all life your ally, all existence,
The powers of water and fire, of air and loam;
As ----muscles and blood, courage and beauty bringing –
You enter in
Be to your lover as the bow singing
Is to the violin.

27 March 1934

Contempt of Court

Contempt, my lord? It's not contempt we feel ;
We, from the age of science and of steel,
Are privileged to view, thus staged, the last
Rite of taboo from our far primitive past.

Your aboriginal innocence forbids
Contempt; your bland blind aspect rids
The enquiring mind of all save anthropology:
Writ, affidavit and apology,

Full-bottomed wig and judge and carefully rounded
Snake-phrases twisting – these will be all confounded
By lazy schoolboys, fifty years from now,
With fetish-reverence and the Sacred Cow.

The Hoodoo-Voodoo Congo's swart attorney
Quotes ancient precedent .... A longer journey
The enquiring mind takes : there was once a time
When even to say a god's name was a crime,

Sacrilege, blasphemy. Now to take yours 'in vain ';
Is worse than that. No penalty or pain
Attends 'their God's an old man and untrue,
Ugly and cruel.' But if 'twas spoken of you …!

1926? and Oct 1934

The Test

*'All highly stressed components must be provided with a test-piece
of appropriate size. This test-piece should remain integral with the
component until all processes except balancing are completed. It should
then be tested to destruction...' Principles of Aero-Engine Design*

Here's a drop-forging: rough, still warm
From its flare-metal birth,
Resilient-rigid, essence of all that earth
Has in it of strength, a mountain's heart distilled
To a metal bar. It shows the form
Of the future crankshaft, as machined and drilled
And cut to knife-edge scantlings, it's trimmed so
The balance-finger moves to a breath's echo.

And after the gouging and the burnishing
And after the arc's heat and the oil douching
Here's a new crankshaft fit to climb the sky,
Tempered, true, ready –
But for one thing :
Shear off this metal square for the final testing !

Past the pressure and the flame
Past the lathe's steel teeth
One with the crankshaft, this our test-piece came
To severance – and death ?
'Test to destruction' – yes, but this can prove
Too hard for twisting, for the impact wheel :
Clean steel,
DIMITROV !

January 1934

Speaking Concretely

A Reply to C. Day Lewis

There's a road building that these times will take,
You and I build. But all hell's length to go
If you and I are separable so –
Water from rock. No : Everyman's fingers, we slake
Hot lime with water, to bind rock ; we make
Concrete for path, bridge-pier, revetment ; grinding
Rubble, stone, sand ; with steel inforcement designing
These strengths into solid no black frost can break.

Marx for your map, Lenin theodolite –
This is a thing Smolny's October shewed –
Crag-contour pioneered, valley and peak's height
Known : all is ready ? No, steel wire must be
Inseparable from concrete, you from me,
We from the durable millions. Then there's a road !

November 1934

Rakosi

Eight years ago the cell shut out
The striding seasons and the sky :
Clean bread ; and work well through, the bite
Of thought that turns thought like a plough ;

The ordinary things men do
That body the strength they have to live ;
The sleep-assuring immediacy
Of human touch a kiss can prove –

Eight years ago. A sick man kicked
With question-threats, it's your voice men
Hear as attacking ; you reject
Excuse, the plea to be forgiven.

Some eager metals, that men keep
Shut airless, brought to air flame like
A shell-burst, blinding ; these, the type
In bone and rock, flare when you speak.

March 1935

A Natural History

When the Greenland great whale, the ship-killer, berg-breaker,
Feels his blood warming with spring-strength, desire-drive,
He lashes, threshes tail, fin ; equinoctial gales
Are signs of the waking fervours of these whales.

Then he begins to swim, furrows a colour-crested water-wave
House-high, whelming; all small waves ship-slapping, beach-
bumping
Everywhere through the world are his wave's ripple-echoes
(Look, ripple-rings from dropped stone.) And he goes
Hill-climbing the earth's curve, Capricorn-Cancer, storm-surging
Down the earth's curve to far sea-fields, sun-strewn,
Lone, lost, shipless; gulf streams and such are back-lifted
Friction-fired steaming seas that he's over-shifted.

Then, when he meets his mate bare-bellied, shining-sided,
Typhoon, earth-quiver, tornado are not stronger-shaking, more
mighty,
Than the weight of their want each for each, than their slow
Quicker, wave-racing, repeated and varied, fall, flow
Each to each. And there's no
Stronger axle for earth to spin round on (eternal – returning
To the dark and the day, sun – shower, flower- frost)
Than the whale's centre-sword, than this living
Flesh of his seeking and getting, his passion and giving.

3 April 1936

Empire Air Day 1936

They are singing a vibrant pattern into the sky,
Moving like bars of music, andante cantabile flying,
Metal tuned to a dance, wind its shape showing :
    This we see, this we know.

Mustard gas, 'dew of death' – poetic, that poison's name –
Froths in the rotted lungs ; as she drowns in the phlegm
A girl tears at her breasts in a writhing labour ;
    That we remember.

The wings lift up, squadron by squadron sweeping,
Beauty and power mix-moulded, feathers of steel :
These we'll make use and pride for mankind, no longer
    blood-dripping ;
    This - we will !

July 1936

We're Going On !

Neither fools nor children any longer;
Those ways, traits, gone and away.
That once made life-a-luck game, death a stranger
We're going on.

Dynamo-driven city waiting bombers
Roadways barricade-unpaved, fear
In the torn minds: the mind remembers
What it's all for.

Death means the corpses warm alive when buried:
Death means the retching brothels where on black
Death's tide, death fear, an army of boys is carried
To a pox wreck.

And life's a matter of beating this, of breaking
By our hardness, and a held hand, out
Of fury, frustration, fear, the waiting, the shouting,
The hate of the fate.

Neither fools nor children, we who are joining
(twenty years ago I knew war's face)
We make what can wreck others into our gaining,
Into our choice.

19 September 1936

Granien - British Medical Unit

Too many people are in love with Death
And he struts thigh-proud, never sleeps alone;
Acknowledge him neighbour and enemy, both
Hated and usual, best avoided when
Best known.

'Weep, weep, weep!' say machine-gun bullets, stating
Mosquito-like, a different note close by;
Hold steady the lamp; the black, the torn flesh lighting
And the glinting probe; carry the stretcher; wait,
Eyes dry.

Our enemies can praise death and adore death;
For us endurance, the sun; and now in the night
This electric torch, feeble, waning, yet close-set,
Follows the surgeon's fingers. We are allied with
This light.

Barcelona, 2 November 1936

International Brigades

Men are tied down, not only by poverty,
By the certain, the usual, the things others do,
By fear for and fear of another. Liberty
Is a silly word, in this flat life, and used
Usually by a Lord Chief Justice. It smells of last century.
There are free men in Europe still :
They're in Madrid.

Men are so tired, running fingers down football tables
Or the ticker-tape, or standing still,
Unemployed, hating street-corners, unable
--Earth-damned, famine-forced, worn grey with worklessness –
To remember man hood and marching, a song or a parable ...

While the free men of Europe
Pile into Madrid.

Men who could not be broken even by Hitler's prisons,
Rubber truncheon, police spy, surrender of friends,
From the Lipari islands, from the divisions
Roadmaking in French Morocco under the sun;
And from comfort, good wages, home – each of them
            made his decision

The free men of Europe, not yet ten thousand,
Raid forward from Madrid.

Forming today the third of the brigades, equipping Italians,
Frenchmen, Germans, Poles, Jugo-Slavs, Greeks,
--The names mean languages only : these are Europeans –
The staff, corduroy-trousered, discuss when Franco will use it:
'Two weeks' or 'a month yet'? How many gas-masks by then?

Will Europe, will England, will you 'have given the gas-masks'
For the free men of Europe
Entrenched in Madrid?

Estado Mayor, Brigada Internacional,
28 November, 1936

'It's a Strange Thing ...'

It's a strange thing to write of love when a world's breaking
Back into poison-gas, shell-shock, the mud death;
When I'm sleeping lonely and cold, it's strange to be speaking
Of a girl I lived with ----

Yes, as far back as that in the past is our loving,
No part of the soldier's life (new life begun
Twenty years – more – ago), yet its colour giving
The light I see life in.

My home's her shoulder and her arm's curve holding
My hand to enclose her breast, and I have known
In a strange far-off past, our bodies' welding
And their release again.

Yet there is one thing, dominant, prevailing,
The key, clue, certainty answer to our pain :
It's possible for two to mingle thought and feeling,
Two eyes, one thing seen.

Albacete, December 1936

January in Spain

Turn of the year, and already I am thinking
Because of lambs seen (first parade, at dawn)
Of a Lincoln sheepfold, Clarke's man walking
Home as the stars thin ;

Already I remember the impatient swinging
Flood-tide at Richmond bridge, my riotous boy
Out on the river-paths, venture-exploring,
Content to be with me.

Yes, we hate England's foulness; we hate London
For its soot-sepulchre, its yellow fat
Sweated out of all the world ; we've got a hand on
Harrow and plough for it;

But never say we hate the English country
Or English folk. How much I'd give to walk
Across the common to a lighted doorway
And tea, and your talk !

9 January 1937

Spanish Lesson

Young men marching, gallant Spanish fashion,
The free arm swinging across and elbow high,
Are Spain's new bread and wine,
The blood of new Spain's passion,
The body of our sacrifice ;
Vino y pan.

Their gesture as they march is that of the peasant
Scattering the rough grain that shall be your bread;
And our hunger, desire
For the grape-breasted vine,
Is Spain's past year and present :
Hambre y sed.

After harvest, after victory, we shall be forgotten
As men forget seed-grain, harrowing, dung –
Blood of wounds gone rotten –
But hope is down the path
Of the young men marching :
Guerra --- y paz

August 1937

Poem in the Summer of 1937

Moving across the field a girl in a pink dress,
Over the sky white clouds shadowed with pink,
Dark on my vision, near to me, your black hair;
While the viola and the voice keep
their lovely argument.
In my hand the spray of elder golden pale
And sweet with summer.

Hay in the meadow cream-folded lies
to darken in the sun, tomorrow and tomorrow,
richening the scent already heavy
in honey loops on the cream taste of summer.
Feasting goes on all day, all night; all senses
Banquet in June, and love uninterrupted
And tireless wakes in morning, sleeps all night,
Rises and sets in the clear skies of joy.

Not uninterrupted. Love is not
Timeless. Love is over
For thousands who went out this summer weather
And found the feast set, and the feast was death.

And these were ours who died.
Dark on my vision your black hair,
So near to me, it shadows all the sun.

August 1937

Monument

When from the deep sky
And digging in the harsh earth,
When by words hard as bullets,
Thoughts simple as death,
You have won victory,
People of Spain,
You will remember the free men who fought beside you,
enduring and dying with you, the strangers
Whose breath was your breath.

You will pile into the deep sky
A tower of dried earth,
Rough as the walls where bullets
Splashed men to death
Before you won victory,
Before you freed Spain
From the eating gangrene of wealth, the grey pus of pride,
the black scab of those strangers
Who were choking your breath.

Bring together, under the deep sky
Metal and earth;
Metal from which you made bullets
And weapons against death,
And earth in which, for victory,
Across all Spain,
Your blood and ours was mingled, Huesca to Malaga;
earth to which your sons and strangers
Gave up the same breath.

Bring to the tower, to its building,
From New Castille,

From Madrid, the indomitable breast-work,
Earth of a flower-bed in the Casa del Campo,
Shell-splinters from University City,
Shell-casing from the Telephonica.
Bring from Old Castille, Santander, Segovia,
Sandbags of earth dug out of our parapets
And a false coin stamped in Burgos by a traitor.

Carry from Leon, from the province of Salamanca,
Where the bulls are brave and the retired generals cowards,
From near the Capital of treason and defeat, bring now
Clean earth, new and untouched, from the cold hills,
And iron from the gate, that shall now be always open
Of Spain's oldest school, where there shall be young wisdom.

From Extramadura, earth from the bullring
Where they shot the prisoners in Badajoz;
And lovely Zafra shall give one of its silver crosses;
Galicia, sea-sand and ship-rivets. From Asturias
Spoil from the pits that taught our dynamiters
To face and destroy the rearing tanks, and a pit-haft
That has cut coal and trenches, and is still fit for work.
From the Basque country, Bilbao, Guernica,
City of agony, villages of fire,
Take charred earth, so burnt and tortured no one
Knows if small children's bones are mingled in it;
Take iron ore from the mines those strangers envied;
And wash your hands, remembering a world that did so.

Navarre shall give a ploughshare and a rock;
Aragon, soil from the trench by the walnut-tree
Where Thaelmann's first group fought towards Huesca,
And steel from a wrecked car lying by a roadside;

Lukacsz rode in that car.
Catalonia, Spain and not Spain, and our gateway
(For myself a gateway to Spain and courage and love)
Shall bring a crankshaft from the Hispano factory
And earth from Durrutti's grave;
Valencia, black soft silt of the rice fields, mingled
With soil from an orange-grove – also
Telephone-wire, and a crane's chain.
Murcia, a surgeon's scalpel and red earth;
Andalucia, the vast south, shall pay
The barrel of a very old rifle found in the hills
Beside a skeleton; earth
That the olives grow from.
And Albacete, where we built our brigades:
Knife-steel and road-dust.

Take then these metals, under the deep sky
Melt them together; take these pieces of earth
And mix them; add your bullets
And memories of death:
You have won victory, People of Spain,
And the tower into which your earth is built, and
    Your blood and ours, shall state Spain's
    Unity, happiness, strength; it shall face the breath
Of the east, of the dawn, of the future, when there will be no more
strangers ...

August – October 1937

Hospital in August

Only the dust-filled wind that drifts and dies
Gives scent or stir or colour. Lying here
Cold and stiff shadowed, long and grey and bare,
Blank walls enclose me. I have memories
Of elm trees whispering, and children's cries ...
Here the one sound's the sick wind 'gainst the fold
Of the sun faded window curtains. Old
And heavy with long watch o'er agonies ...

The long hours lying wounded in the sun –
The ache and throb and rattle of the train –
The weariness of waiting and the pain –
Little are these besides a tortured mind,
Recalling how to cool streams swift feet run,
Naked and free and restless as the wind.

August 1937

The Splint

Time stops when the bullet strikes,
Or moves to a new rhyme:
No longer measured by the eyes'
Leap, pulse-beat, thought-flow,
Minutes are told by the jerked wound,
By the pain's throb, fear of pain, sin
Of giving in,
And the unending hardness of the pillow.

Hours in the night creep at you like enemy
Patrols, quiet-footed: powers
And pretences that are yourself give way
As without sound the
Splint bites tighter; there are still
Four hours to dawn: why is it a sin
To moan, to give in?
There is no answer from the bitter pillow.

But there's an answer, back of your thoughts,
Can keep mind and mouth shut:
Can, if you'll hear it, release you. These men
Count you a man:
In and because of their friendship you can remember
One who's the world's width away: can think
To moan, to give in,
Would waken the curved girl who shares your pillow.

Benacasim and St Thomas Hospital September – December 1937

Embarkation Leave

For each embarkation leave
in the changing war that is never over
while we have lives,
we have the need to state our need.

We've both known love as a wound's fever;
known, too, the words 'it isn't loaded'
that are suicide;
and there's plenty left of childhood's greed;

So this loving's possible, and no other:
bodies delight in beating death ---
no fool hope's growth,
none of the waiting, the futile grieving.

We need the sunlight's unhurried loving
that pauses for laughter, or for breath,
but takes no oath.
Is it impossible. So is our living.

Notes

The text of the poems is based on papers in the Wintringham Archive in the Liddell Hart Centre for Military Archives at Kings College, London University.

30p Lord Roberts of Kandahar VC ('Father Bobs' in Kipling's phrase), visited Gresham's School not long before his death.

33p This poem draws on Edgar Allen Poe's *A Descent into the Maelstrom*, a whirling abyss of water off the Lofoten Islands near Norway.

34p Utterby Pines are a few miles from Grimsby.

36p 'Thoughts come like shadow unseen...', 'Within my heart...' and 'When Death's Swift Fingers...' appear to have been written for a boy at Gresham's named Frederick Taylor.

42p 'Dawn Near Vimy' and 'Below Vimy' were written over a year apart and refer to two quite separate actions. The first was the capture of Vimy Ridge by the Allies in April 1917, in which the Second Kite Balloon Corps distinguished itself, and the second was between Arras and Bethune after Ludendorff's offensive a year later.

46p Shortly after the armistice Wintringham crashed his motorbike in Northern France and ended up in hospital at Newton Abbott in Devon. After the War the Allies continued to starve German civilians by a naval blockade untill Germany agreed peace terms.

47p 'To Margaret, In Her Fifth Summer' and 'Margaret' were written for Wintringham's favourite sister, Meg, born in 1913. For the 'small French miss' see Wintringham's story 'First Love' in *New Writing* in 1936.

52p 'the silver tree/ That stands by Trinity gate' is the tree that Isaac Newton sat under when the apple fell and he worked out the theory of gravity.

55p Published in the *Sunday Worker* 17 January 1926, when Wintringham was still in prison.

57p 'The promise' was Baldwin's £10 million subsidy to the coal industry that came to an end on 1 May 1926.

59p Wintringham spent six months in prison, mostly in Wandsworth, between November 1925 and April 1926. He was employed in the prison library (traditionally a sanctuary for intellectual revolutionaries).

61p Wintringham's wife Elizabeth was also a member of the Communist Party.

62p Wintringham's firstborn child, Robin, died in 1928.

64p Published in *Storm* February 1933. This short-lived magazine defined itself as 'a virile and progressive counter-blast to the reams of counter-revolutionary dope' and 'the thoughts and actions of the decaying bourgeoisie'.

66p 'Earth, Air, Fire and Water', 'We Quarrel So About Politics' and 'Be To Your Lover' were written during Wintringham's affair with Millie ; 'Earth, Air, Fire and Water' celebrates the conception of their daughter Lesley, born in September 1931.

69p Published in the first issue of *Left Review* October 1934. In 1931 Mr Justice Rigby Swift sentenced three Communists to between eight and eighteen months in prison for writing 'revolutionary pamphlets' aimed at the armed forces. When the *Daily Worker* called Judge Swift 'a bewigged puppet', the business manager was sent down for nine months on a charge of contempt of court. Swift was the same judge who in 1925 had offered Wintringham the choice of leaving the Communist Party or six months in prison.

70p First published in *Labour Monthly* March 1934. Georgi Dimitrov was a Bulgarian Communist and hero of the Reichstag Trial. He later became General Secretary of the Comintern and launched the Popular Front at the Seventh Congress the next year.

71p Published in *Left Review* November 1934 ; it was a reply to C. Day Lewis' 'The Road These Times Must Take', which appeared in the same issue of the magazine.

72p Published in *Left Review* March 1935. Mathias Rakosi was a Hungarian, Jewish Communist. A member of Bela Kun's short lived Soviet regime in Hungary, he had just finished eight years in solitary confinement under Hungary's semi-fascist regime. Shortly after Wintringham wrote this poem, Rakosi was sent back to prison for life. He became Stalin's puppet leader of Hungary after the Second World War.

74p Published in *Left Review* July 1936. Two months earlier the Italians has used poison gas in their invasion of Abyssinia.

75p Published in *Volunteer for Liberty* I no 23 and Stephen Spender and John Lehmann (eds) *Poems for Spain* as 'Barcelona Nerves' ; the MS is dated 'For KB: 2.30am 19/9/36'.

76p Published in *Left Review* January 1937 as 'British Medical Unit - Grañen', later in *Volunteer for Liberty* I no 24 and *Poems for Spain* (1939) ; the MS is dated '2/11/36 "With my love to my Shrimp. T"' ('Shrimp' was Wintringham's name for Kitty). The hospital at Granien was on the way to the Aragon front north west of Barcelona. It was the base of the British Medical Unit with which he had travelled out to Spain.

77p Wintringham wrote this shortly after he had been commissioned as a machine-gun instructor to the American, Franco-Belge and British battalions.

79p This poem was written for Millie when Wintringham was training the British Battalion at Albacete.

80p   This poem was addressed to Elizabeth.

83p   Published in *Left Review* October 1937. Wintringham was hit by a sniper's bullet on the 25 August 1937. He was moved by train to hospital at Benicasim, where he wrote this poem. Wintringham was in the same ward as the writer Gustav Regler, then a senior political commissar in the International Brigades, but shortly to leave the German Communist Party. Regler had spent the previous year in Moscow, where he had witnessed the trials of Zinoviev and Kamenev (both known personally to Wintringham). Although Wintringham's hospital letters to Kitty were censored, it is clear that the two wounded men talked a great deal about the role of the Comintern in Spain. Burgos was General Franco's administrative headquarters. Salamanca was the capital where Franco and the foreign embassies were based. The Nationalists captured Badajoz in August 1936 and slaughtered up to 2,000 militiamen fighting for the Republic. The Catholic priest of Zafra was notoriously bloodthirsty; on one occasion he ordered that a captured militiamen and a wounded girl should dig their own graves and then be buried alive. On 26 April 1937 Guernica was bombed by the Nazi Condor Legion and became the subject of Picasso's iconic painting. The Thaelmann (German) Centuria was the first foreign militia to fight with the Republic. Wintringham watched them in action in September 1936 and was further convinced of the need for an international brigade. Mata Lukacs was a Hungarian general in the International Brigades, killed by the bomb which injured Gustav Regler. Durrutti was a formidable, violent Anarchist. He was killed in Madrid on 20 November 1936 and buried in Barcelona in front of 200,000 mourners.

86p   Wintringham was wounded in the shoulder while the XV Brigade was capturing Quinto, a little village in the Ebro valley. He was hit on only his second day after returning to action; he had been wounded on the second day of Jarama too. His first wound had been to his thigh. This one was more serious. His shoulder bone had been splintered and one particular splinter extended almost down to his elbow and became infected. He required two operations in Spain and a third in England, in between which he was heavily bandaged. When he was repatriated in early November his brother hardly recognised him: 'He looked as if he had been dead and buried for six or seven weeks'.

'Smokestack has a great squad of radical poets
lined up for its first season. I predict that the
team will roll like thunder, strike like lightning
and electrify British poetry.'

Adrian Mitchell

PO Box 408, Middlesbrough TS5 6WA
Tel:01642813997
e-mail: info@smokestack-books.co.uk
w w w . s m o k e s t a c k - b o o k s . c o . u k
21. March. 06

Dear Michael,

Here are the Smokestack titles I promised you.
I hope you like them, especially the Cwistenyham
Herne and Seattle. It would be great if you
could mention the Smokestack project in Political
Affairs. Did you ever run a review. I feel slights at Night?

Best wishes.

Andy C.

87p   Published in *Poems for Spain* and *Penguin New Writing* April 1942.

88p Published in *Penguin New Writing* July 1946.